CW00506513

PAIN
INTO
POWER

**TRANSFORM YOUR PATTERN OF PAIN
THOUGH THE POWER OF YOUR
MINDBODY CONNECTION**

JAKKIE TALMAGE

" YOUR PAIN IS THE KEY TO YOUR HEALING "

DEEPAK CHOPRA

Copyright © 2023 by Jakkie Talmage

Published by LightWorks
Interview by Tamara Norwood
Edited by Jodie Richards
Design by Jakkie Talmage

What is your pain trying to tell you?

This revolutionary book will help you understand your pain, be it emotional or physical, in a whole new way.

You'll discover your MindBody Connection and learn how to uncover old patterns of pain and reprogram your mind, so you can live a life free from pain and struggle. In the process, you may even discover the real reason why you're reading this book.

the author

Jakkie Talmage has worked with bodies for over 25 years and has witnessed miraculous transformations in the body by healing the pain of the past.

She challenges many of our default thought patterns around pain and how it can be cured.

Although Jakkie is extremely intuitive and helps people to heal in a way no one else does, this book is very grounded, giving clear practical answers based on science, helping even the non-believer to transform their pain into their power.

Discover
the power of your
MindBody Connection
with Jakkie Talmage

Jakkie, tell us how you first discovered the MindBody connection: why's healing pain so important to you and how did you become so committed to helping people understand that there's an alternative way to healing pain?

It started in 1995 when I was training as a massage therapist. One of my first clients was a Buddhist nun suffering from back pain. She came for a massage once a week for three months and never missed a session. She'd take off her orange robes, lie on the massage couch, and as soon as I laid my hands on her, she'd start to cry. She never uttered a word during our sessions; she just sobbed and sobbed.

At first, I was alarmed by her tears and wondered what was going on. Was I hurting her? Was I upsetting her? Was she having some sort of breakdown? I wanted to ask her a million questions, but something inside me knew I needed to trust that she knew what she was doing, and so I just let her cry.

To my relief, on the 12th week she didn't cry during our session. Afterward, she said, "Thank you, Jakkie. I don't need to see you again because I'm no longer in pain".

Years later, I came across an article about her in the local newspaper. In the article he told her moving story, explaining

13

how she'd naturally healed herself of breast cancer.

This incredible event helped me to understand that when I massaged my clients to release their muscle pain, I was also healing them on a deeper level. At the time, this was something I didn't quite understand.

After many years of working with bodies, patterns started to emerge. I kept seeing clients with similar physical symptoms and the same corresponding psycho-emotional issues. It was becoming clear to me that the mind and emotion were inextricably linked to physical pain, and I was eager to learn more. And so, I embarked upon a lifelong journey exploring the MindBody connection. I discovered that the mind, body, emotions, and spirit are an intricate, intelligent network that works together, subconsciously, and not separate entities.

Once I discovered how incredibly powerful the subconscious connection between mind and body was, I set about designing a 12-week course called *Your MindBody Journey*.

I wanted other people to experience first-hand the power of their own MindBody connection and teach them to consciously use it to become healthy, happy, and empowered.

the journey begins

To test my theories, I offered the course free to clients, friends, and anyone willing to be my guinea pig. I was astounded by both the results and the feedback. In just 12 sessions, I'd managed to help participants shift lifelong suffering and begin their own healing journey.

The second time I ran the course, it was so overbooked that I had to run two back-to-back to accommodate everyone. Only then did I truly comprehend that teaching the MindBody connection, could empower people to heal themselves!

I wanted to share this knowledge with a larger audience, so I rewrote the course in book format and published *Your MindBody Journey.*

I'm passionate about helping others break free from emotional, and physical patterns of pain, so they can live the happy, healthy lives they truly deserve.

How do we experience pain?

None of us want pain, but unfortunately it's part of the human experience. It can be emotional, mental, spiritual, and/or physical. We generally recover quickly from short bursts of pain, but when pain is persistent, it can be utterly debilitating. I get it because I've been there!

The physical pain of a traumatic injury, severe illness or physical abuse isn't only experienced physically; there will also be emotional pain associated with the incident. This can turn into trauma if we emotionally become attached to the story of the incident.

Emotional pain can be caused by those big life events that affect us deeply—loss, grief, betrayal, and/or separation. But it can also be caused by little day-to-day grievances or upsets that trigger us relentlessly. For example: if you're unable to forgive someone for hurting you, the emotional pain associated with the hurt will persist.

Mental pain can result from depression, anxiety, or fear. To compound matters, thinking about depression, anxiety and fear increases depression, anxiety, and fear, creating a psycho-emotional pain loop. This overloads the brain and takes a toll on the body's adrenals.

Spiritual pain is felt if we sense we have no purpose or place in the world. When we experience spiritual pain, we don't know who we are or what we want—we feel lost, alone, separate, confused, and disempowered.

If I suspect someone is experiencing spiritual pain, I will ask questions like:

'Do you feel like you've lost your way in life?'
'Do you repeat the same struggles?'
'Do you attract co-dependent relationships?'
'Do you feel like no one really 'get's' you?'

If you were nodding your head to any of those questions, it could indicate that you're in spiritual pain.

What's a psycho-emotional pain loop?

The pain loop can drive us crazy! That's why it's important to understand it so that we can break free from it.

We all experience pain differently, depending on the intensity of it, our attachment to it, and our interpretation of it. Mind and emotion can feed off each other in a never-ending cycle.

For instance, if we think about our pain, we automatically feel an emotion related to our thoughts about the pain; the more the pain is thought about, the more that emotion is fuelled; and the more emotional we feel, the more we think about it; resulting in what's known as a psycho-emotional pain loop.

Psycho-emotions are feelings triggered by the mind, and if you're stuck in a psycho-emotional pain loop, you can feel like it's taking over your life. Sometimes the loop is so deep that it even takes lives.

But pain speaks to us clearly, if we take the time to listen to it. Your pain is your inner guidance system, telling you where you need healing. Pain calls us to examine our lives and offers a pathway to love, peace, health, and happiness. That's why understanding the MindBody connection is so empowering. It definitely transformed my life!

Why do some people feel they're not getting better using Western Medicine?

Unfortunately, the western health care system is an "illness system," in that it focuses on illness rather than wellness. The modern medical model generally only treats the body once it's sick and doesn't prescribe preventative measures to keep the body healthy.

Furthermore, western medical practitioners only look at the body for answers to medical issues. They aren't trained to look at the physical body in conjunction with the emotional, mental, and spiritual health of the patient. They treat the body's symptoms without investigating the root cause of the illness. And because as individuals we aren't encouraged to investigate the root cause, we don't, which keeps us sick.

By contrast, eastern practitioners tend to look at the whole body to find a healing solution. They understand the body as a holistic energy system, with energy centres and pathways that are influenced by the environment, our thoughts, our beliefs, and our experiences. If this energy is overactive, underactive or a pathway is blocked, the body will react with discomfort, pain and/or disease.

In the west, we've been taught that pharmaceutical drugs are the solution to most health issues. So, it's easy to forget that the human body is an incredible self-healing mechanism—biologically programmed to repair itself!

Taking drugs, ironically, disrupts and deactivates the body's natural healing systems. Drugs might be a good short-term fix, but other symptoms are likely to appear because the cause hasn't been addressed. Typically, these new symptoms will be treated with drugs, creating a vicious illness cycle. If the root cause of a condition isn't uncovered and healed, health issues will continue regardless of drug regimens or physical treatments.

Don't get me wrong, modern medicine offers huge advantages. Technology provides us with reliable diagnoses, skilled surgeons perform life-saving operations, and we've never lived so long. But the picture is far bigger, and if modern medical practitioners are unwilling to look at the root cause of our health issues, then it falls to each of us to take responsibility and ownership of our wellbeing with a combination of holistic approaches and modern medicine.

it's best to express

A close friend of mine had reoccurring UTIs and severe eczema—often at the same time—and used a cocktail of drugs and lotions to treat the conditions. Flare-ups occurred whenever she was angry or upset.

Because we're close, I know she finds it hard to express emotions and tends to bottle everything up. She grew up with strict parents, who chastised her whenever she cried or shouted. Deep in her subconscious, she believed that if she expressed her raw emotions, she'd be punished. As a consequence, she subconsciously learned to suppress her feelings to avoid punishment.

However, the energy of emotion must go somewhere, and her unexpressed emotional energy found an outlet through her skin (with eczema) and her bladder (with UTIs). Once she understood this, she worked on feeling safe to express her emotions freely. Over time, expressing herself authentically resolved her repeated pain patterns, clearing the UTIs and eczema.

Changing deeply entrenched patterns takes commitment and perseverance. For some people, transformation is miraculous, but for others it's like learning to un-ride a bike! My friend, for example, still occasionally gets UTIs and eczema, but whenever they flare up, she knows the cause and is empowered to deal with it.

What are the most common misconceptions when it comes to physical pain?

The most common misconception when it comes to physical pain is that it's a purely physical issue, created in the present moment. Typically, we believe a physical issue can only be fixed with physical therapy, drugs, surgery, or another physical solution. The psycho-emotional aspect is rarely addressed when discussing physical pain.

Some time ago, Dianna came to see me with hip pain, so severe that she often spent most of the day in bed. She was a single mum to three small children, so it was a struggle to look after them effectively.

She had scans, massages, chiropractic treatments and acupuncture, but nothing would shift the pain. During our conversation, she informed me that she'd had three traumatic childbirths and that during one, she almost died from a severe haemorrhage.

I identified unreleased trauma stuck in her hip and together we started to energetically move the stuck trauma down her leg and out her foot.

"It was like giving birth all over again—the pain was excruciating," she said. But once the trauma had been released her hip pain completely vanished.

patterns of pain

Our muscles have memory and store information like a computer. This is why you remember how to ride a bike. Bike riding is part of your muscular memory.

Have you ever experienced driving a new car and instead of putting on the indicator, you put the windscreen wipers on instead? Our body has learnt that the indicator is on the left and not the right, even though we have been told that the new car has the opposite setup, we still can't break free from our old programming.

In the same way, the body holds onto unresolved physical and emotional pain, programming it into muscular memory. When triggered, the computer runs the program that's been installed in muscular memory, playing out an old pain.

Our bodies are living, walking, and talking mechanisms of memory, programmed by our experiences from conception up to this very moment. We even genetically carry patterns of pain from our parents and grandparents in our cells. To fully understand our bodies, we must take into account all of our past: our experiences, our memories, our conditioning, and our ancestors' patterns.

Your body is a map of your life so far, so when it comes to physical pain, it's important to see the bigger picture.

What's the most common misconception when it comes to emotional pain?

The most common misconception when it comes to emotional pain is that your pain IS you. Some people identify themselves as their pain, crafting the story of who they are with their pain as the centrepiece. Emotional pain becomes a constant companion, and it defines some people's lives.

Negative emotions are an indication that an old emotional pain has been triggered. We all have triggers—things that make us upset or angry and cause us to react emotionally. Blaming others for our emotional outbursts, instead of taking responsibility for them, squanders a golden opportunity for deep healing.

How do triggers work?

A trigger is when someone or something makes you angry, hurt, or upset. It's usually a repeating theme, and it indicates a deep, unhealed wound. When someone or something scratches the surface of a wound, we react by blaming instead of addressing the source of the pain.

Family members are particularly good at triggering us. That's why, despite loving them dearly, they infuriate the hell out of us!

In my own relationship, I'd often be triggered by the same things, which sent me into a spiral of emotional pain. I was usually triggered when I wanted something done my way, but my partner would carry on doing it his way. This would make me feel undervalued, unsupported, undermined, and unloved, and the more I insisted my needs be met, the more he'd dig his heels in.

This pattern of pain is one we'd find ourselves in quite regularly. It was horrid to live in this kind of relationship, and it almost split us up. Thankfully, we discovered why the pattern kept reoccurring and broke the torturous loop.

I had an authoritarian father and was always told what to do.

My need to be heard wasn't met as a child, which made me feel undervalued, unsupported, undermined, and unloved. So, as an adult, I tried to gain more control over my needs.

On the other hand, my partner had been constantly manipulated and controlled by the dominant females in his life, including his mother, big sister, and ex-wife. He was highly sensitive when he believed he was being manipulated and controlled.

We were locked in this pattern of struggle for many years until we understood why we behaved and reacted the way we did. This freed us completely, and I'm happy to report that it's no longer an issue in our lives.

So, when you find yourself being triggered, ask yourself;
'How is this making me feel?'
'What need is not being fulfilled?'
'What belief do I have about myself because of this?'
'When did this false belief about myself begin?'

Understanding your MindBody connection will empower you to break free from old, destructive patterns of pain.

pain is the
pathway to power

Your pain is the pathway to your power. Once you understand the root cause of your pain, it's transformed into the gift of insight. Instead of being its victim, your emotional pain becomes a gateway to the life you know—deep within—you deserve.

Why are most of your clients experiencing pain?

Many of my clients come to see me to help manage their muscle pain. Most of the time, muscle manipulation, coupled with identifying and changing the repetitive habit causing their pain, is enough to get them on their way again. However, when the pain doesn't go away, I can often see a psycho-emotional root cause.

Unfortunately, most people aren't particularly open to this concept, so I can't help them resolve their issues at a root level and, consequently, the pain comes back. Once they're ready to explore their deeper wounds, that's when the healing can really begin.

Melody came to see me because of a pain in her left shoulder and neck. When I examined her body, she had a hardened lump of muscle sitting by her shoulder blade (rhomboids). This lump referred up into her neck restricting her blood flow. No wonder she was in so much pain.

Initially I treated her muscle with a few sessions of remedial massage, but each time I broke down the calcified lump, it just kept coming back. It was then I realised we needed to dig a little deeper to find the reason as to why it wouldn't heal.

I explained to her that shoulders represent responsibility, feeling like the world is on your shoulders. Neck issues represent the need to be in control. This information triggered a deep truth within her and she started to cry.

She confessed that she was an over controlling mum and wife. When I asked her why she believed she was like this, she said, 'Because I'm so frightened of anything happening to my kids'. 'Like what?' I asked. 'Accidents' she said.

'When do you think this belief started? Did anything happen to you as a child?' I asked.

She then she broke down and sobbed.

When Melody was 7, she had a 2-year-old baby brother. The whole family were picnicking by a lake one day and Melody took her little brother off for a walk around the lake. Mandy got side-tracked by a butterfly that had landed on her. The next minute when she looked up, her baby brother was in the water, up to his neck about to drown. Luckily the parents saw this and intervened quickly. Her brother was fine, but she wasn't, because from that day, she felt responsible for his near fatal accident and has been over cautious ever since.

'It's time to let go of the reins', I said

As I continued to work on her shoulder her arms started to jerk and shake in odd ways. I knew this was her body letting go of the past, so I encouraged her to allow her body to do whatever it needed. After the treatment, her eyes looked bright, her face was soft, and she was smiling.

Once she was back in her life, whenever she felt the old issue of control kicking in, she would chant the words, 'I let go and trust'. As a result, she now feels a freedom she hasn't felt since the age of 7. Her shoulder pain has also now gone.

listen to the whispers

When an issue in our lives hasn't properly healed, the body signals this to the brain with pain. At first, these signals may be subtle—our intuition tells us that something doesn't feel quite right. If we ignore this inner knowing, the whispers become shouts. Accidents, injuries, pain and crises are signals for us to stop and examine what's not working in our lives. Looking beneath the physical pain to find a psycho-emotional root cause takes courage, but if the root cause isn't dealt with, the pain will keep coming back.

Pushing through pain, rather than acknowledging it, is a common mistake. I know a marathon runner who's riddled with arthritis and in a great deal of pain. His body screams for him to STOP RUNNING, but he keeps running marathon-after-marathon.

I asked him why he resisted his body's clear messages to stop? He admitted that he was scared of getting old, losing his body shape, and not staying fit, strong, and young. His fear of getting old kept him locked in a cycle of pain. Willpower can easily override pain if we let it.

Ironically, the runner is honouring his psychological need to feel young by running marathons. His challenge, now that he understands his underlying need, is to find a way to meet that need without running marathons and destroying his body.

Our subconscious mind uses very clever strategies to get our emotional needs met. In my own case, my mum attentively nursed me back to health when I was sick as a child. I loved the attention I got when I wasn't well, I certainly didn't receive that level of attention when I was well! My subconscious remembered this.

Now as an adult, whenever I overwork and forget to nurture myself, I get sick. I now know that my subconscious makes me physically sick in order to meet my psycho-emotional need to feel nurtured. It took decades for me to admit to this pattern, but when my body cries out in pain now, I know that I'm not getting the love and attention I crave.

Once the root cause is uncovered, the emotional need is understood and, once met, the pain often stops because it's no longer required.

finding the true story

If you're experiencing patterns of physical pain, it's helpful to examine the emotional needs underpinning that pain. During your examination, you might ask yourself these types of questions:

- Do I feel unworthy of health, love, and/or happiness?
- Do I need to rest and take time off?
- Have I been neglecting myself?
- Have I been punishing myself or those around me?
- Do I feel resentful about giving too much or receiving too little?
- Have I properly grieved a loss?
- Do I feel unsupported?
- Am I suppressing anger or rage?
- Do I crave love and attention?
- Am I fearful of my future?
- Am I avoiding confrontation?
- Do I find it difficult to express my needs?
- Do I have unfulfilled dreams that I'm neglecting?

The list of potential unconscious emotional needs is infinite, but if you listen carefully to the whispers, you'll be guided to your truth.

What's the MindBody Connection?

Most of us have heard the words 'mind-body connection', but for most of us it's a mystery as to what it means! In a nutshell, this is how it works: The mind and body are parts of a unified system. The mind is directly linked to the nervous system, and the nervous system is directly linked to the body. Therefore, every thought causes a reaction within the body. The MindBody connection describes how our bodies respond to our thoughts.

For example, if you think of biting into a juicy lemon, your mouth starts to salivate and your lips purse. If you think about an upcoming exam or an important meeting, you get butterflies in your stomach. Even thinking about walking into a freezer can make you shiver.

The same applies to memories. When you think of a memory, a biochemical reaction begins in your brain causing the brain to release certain chemical signals. These chemical signals make your body feel exactly the way you did in your memory.

Once you notice you are feeling a particular way, then you generate more thoughts equal to how you're feeling, and then you release more chemicals from your brain to make you feel the way you've been thinking. Even though it is a memory that happened in the past, your body believes it is happening now.

When you fire and wire the same circuits in your brain over and over again - because you keep thinking the same thoughts - you are hardwiring your brain into the same patterns. As a result, your brain becomes a replica of your past thinking and in time you automatically think in the same ways. That's why we keep repeating the same patterns of health, emotions, relationships, and experiences in general.

Why do humans have a MindBody Connection?

The MindBody Connection is very useful, in fact it was a life saver! It evolved to keep us safe. It's part of intuition or instinct and is linked to the fight or flight mechanism. If you have a fearful thought, your heart rate quickens, your breathing gets faster, and your palms sweat.

These reactions indicate that your fight, flight, and freeze hormones have automatically activated.

When danger is perceived, the hypothalamus, pituitary, and adrenal systems are instantly triggered to prepare the body for action. The sympathetic nervous system kicks in, releasing adrenalin from the adrenal cortex and cortisone into our bodies to help deal with the danger, and the thyroid gland sends oxygenated blood to the large muscles and vital organs.

It sounds exhausting, but it happens instantly.

Unlike our ancestors, the perils we face don't often include fleeing from a sabre-toothed tiger, but our minds are still biologically wired to respond to that type of danger. If we perceive a threat, it triggers a physical fear-based (fight or flight) response, and, even if the threat is trivial or imagined, our bodies still believe we're in imminent danger.

The other day, I almost had a heart attack when I mistook the hose for a snake!

The body doesn't know the difference between fantasy and reality; it responds to thoughts (real and imagined) the same way. Repetitive anxious or negative thoughts about the future or the past send the nervous system into a hyper-stress response. This often results in adrenal fatigue.

Over time, stress hormones in the body deplete the immune system, resulting in pain, headaches, tight muscles that affect posture, cause organ malfunctions, and glandular issues, which (if left unchecked) lead to more serious illnesses.

We're so used to experiencing stress that we often don't realize we're in a hyper-stress state. Fatigue is "normal" for many of us, so it's good to be aware of the common causes of modern-day stress to help us establish our boundaries.

Some common stress triggers are:

- Watching the news,
- Traffic,
- Noise,
- Work deadlines,
- Phone calls,
- Constant phone alerts: texts, emails, messages, social media,
- Other people's Facebook or Instagram posts,
- Family responsibilities,
- Bills,
- Other people's dramas,

- Worrying about others, and
- Relationship discords.

No matter how trivial the cause of the stress, the body reacts to a sabre-toothed tiger attack. It thinks it's in constant danger because the stress messages from the brain don't let up. And there's only so much stress that our bodies can take before they start to show signs of distress and fatigue.

A plethora of research proves that if we consciously generate loving, happy, peaceful thoughts, it activates a positive immune response in our bodies. So, while the MindBody connection happens automatically, we have control over the messages our brains send to our bodies. What we think matters!

How can we master our MindBody connection?

Unfortunately, most of us have lost connection to our inner wisdom and innate intuition that helps us access our MindBody connection. The modern world doesn't encourage listening to intuitive, feminine, right-brain thinking. It prefers listening to the rational problem-solving, masculine, left-brain.

These traditionally masculine principles have dominated the feminine for the last 2000 years. But, as we leave the Age of Pisces, (1-2000 AD) we leave behind the qualities of materialism, systematic processes, power, and control. And, as we enter the age of Aquarius, we'll embrace the qualities of democracy, freedom, cooperation, and unification.

Now is the time to balance the ledger by giving our masculine and feminine energies equal weight. It's time to redevelop our intuitive skills in line with our analytical skills. Mastering the MindBody connection requires drawing on those feminine intuitive qualities to dig into the psyche, then using our structured masculine minds to rewire repetitive patterns of pain.

Family and work pressures, and the distraction of social media, make finding the time to tune into ourselves and find out what's going on at a deeper level, difficult to achieve. It's easier to ignore the elephant in the room and mask it with alcohol, drugs, sex, overeating, and blaming others.

Ultimately, it's fear that prevents us from listening to our intuition. Change is scary, and discovering the truth is even scarier, and because of this, we get stuck in patterns of pain.

To truly transform our pain patterns and rewire our MindBody connection to one which is healthy and positive, requires a deep desire, conscious intent, and dedication.

It's a choice as to whether we stay disempowered or empowered. I know which one I'd choose!

whatever we resist, persists

Digging bravely for the truth behind pain and suffering is the first step to healing.

Ben, an accomplished squash player, came to me with a torn rotator cuff in his right shoulder. As I massaged the shoulder, I asked him why he thought he had this injury. He looked at me blankly and said, "because I tore it playing squash."

I tried another tack and asked him what shoulders represented to him.

"Burdens," he replied.

"Do you feel burdened?" I asked.

He went silent for a moment and said, "I suppose I feel like I'm shouldering the burden of a secret from a long time ago." On his death bed, his father had asked him to promise to look after his stepbrother. Still in his teens, Ben promised he would, even though he never really got along with his stepbrother. He found it hard to fulfil this promise and felt ashamed and guilty.

I noted that Ben's physical injury was on his right side, as is often the case with 'masculine' burdens. I asked him if he ever took his shame and guilt onto the squash court. "All the time," he said. "There isn't a day that passes when I don't feel like I've let my father down."

After the treatment, I suggested that he make peace with this burden—to either forgive himself for not fulfilling his promise or to fulfil it.

A few months later, Ben informed me that he'd contacted his stepbrother. He told him about the promise, spoke of his guilt, and said he was sorry. His stepbrother was touched by his honesty, and they are now in regular contact.

Ben said he felt different; "free and untroubled". He was also pleased that his shoulder was so much better, his squash game was back to its usual standard, and he had won the last three tournaments!

Jakkie, have you ever achieved great results with a non-believer?

When people are ready to heal on a deeper level, they're generally open to the idea that changing subconscious brain patterns and beliefs can change health patterns. But that's not always the case.

just like magic

Karen came to see me to treat her ongoing back pain. She'd been seeing a chiropractor and, although she got some relief after each session, her back pain kept returning. Once she shared her story with me, it was clear her personal life was contributing to her pain. She felt undervalued, unloved, and unappreciated by everybody in her life.

"I feel like I'm bending over backward for everyone and absolutely nobody appreciates it," she said.

She was locked in an unconscious belief pattern. She believed that if she gave more to others, she'd receive love and validation back. And when she didn't receive what she believed she deserved, she felt resentful, angry, and unloved. Together we released the pattern of pain and introduced a new pattern that would serve her needs. Overnight, her pain vanished and a new pattern prevented it from coming back. Her chiropractor insisted on knowing how I did it. When she told him I hadn't even touched her, he dismissed her claims outright. When someone isn't ready, even compelling evidence won't change their mind.

What is pain according to the MindBody Connection?

There's a complex interplay between the mind and body when we experience pain. Receptors on the skin trigger a series of events, beginning with an electrical impulse that travels from the skin to the spinal cord. The spinal cord acts as a sort of relay centre where the pain signal can be blocked, enhanced, or otherwise modified before it's relayed to the brain.

The most common destination for pain signals is the thalamus. The thalamus serves as the brain's storage area for images of the body. That's why people who have limbs amputated still feel them; the image memory of the amputated limb is still stored in the thalamus. It plays a key role in relaying messages between the brain and various parts of the body.

From the thalamus, signals go to the cortex, which is the headquarters for complex thoughts. Chemicals transmit the pain message by stimulating neurotransmitter receptors found on the surface of cells—each receptor has a corresponding neurotransmitter. These receptors allow pain messages to pass through and into neighbouring cells.

Pain messages can also call for the release of natural painkillers, such as serotonin, norepinephrine, and opioid-like chemicals. Although these processes typically occur unconsciously, it's possible to consciously release natural pain-reducing chemicals.

the real heal

The placebo effect is a well-known example of the mind activating the body's self-healing capacity. In placebo experiments, a group of patients with the same illness all believe they're receiving a curative treatment. However, 50%

are given a sugar pill instead of the cure. In far too many cases for logic to explain, those on the sugar pill are miraculously cured.

In David Hamilton's book, *How Your Mind Can Heal Your Body,* he talks about a placebo experiment with Parkinson's patients. Brain scans of his patients proved that the area of the brain responsible for movement was more active and dopamine levels were elevated, regardless of whether the patient received the active ingredient or the sugar pill. Furthermore, all the participants in the experiment were demonstrably more mobile.

The same research has been duplicated for various conditions and illnesses, and the results are always the same—the brain stimulates the body to produce chemicals tailor-made to combat that particular illness.

However, the placebo effect is a double-edged sword and believing you're sick, will make you sick—this is known as the nocebo effect. Chemicals released to attack an imaginary disease will attack healthy cells, causing problems such as autoimmune disorders.

Joe Dispenza, an American neuroscientist, has dedicated his

life to the study of the MindBody connection. He conducted an experiment with 40 chronically ill participants. Four times a day, for 15 minutes, he asked them to trade their negative emotions (fear, anger, impatience, resentment, etc.) with thoughts and feelings of gratitude. Each time they did this, he measured the chemical reactions within their bodies. The participants produced 50% more of a chemical called IgA (a natural anti-viral and anti-bacterial agent), the thymus gland strengthened, the heart pumped at a healthier rhythm, healing hormones were produced, and the immune system was activated.

think well

Our actions, thoughts, and feelings affect our biology and can make us well or sick. Destructive thoughts (like fear, sadness, resentment, and jealousy) recreate past emotional experiences which manifest in our body's nervous system and create cycles of pain.

The same old thoughts recreate the same old emotions that feed the same old psycho-emotional loop. Changing what you think, changes the way you feel, which changes your body chemistry.

To reprogram negative thoughts, they need to be caught before they trigger an emotional response. Once caught, a negative thought should be starved of energy—pay it no attention at all. Don't accept it or believe it—ignore it.

Breaking the old thought habit will weaken the binding receptors, known as "fire and wire receptors," in the brain. By un-memorising negative emotions and replacing them with new positive emotions, we rewire the brain and change body chemistry. Replacing your bicycle with a unicycle means that you don't actually need to learn to un-ride a bike, you just need to become stronger at riding a unicycle than a bicycle.

Our beliefs and attitudes reshape our cells and bones. Our bodies rebuild themselves constantly. Every second, seven million red blood cells die and re-form. Every four days, we grow a new stomach lining. Every four hundred days the liver cells are replaced. Every seven years, our bones are fully re-built.

The same attitudes and thoughts can only recreate the same body. If we change the way we think and see the world, we can transform our cells and create a new body.

This is how powerful we are!

How does the MindBody Connection affect our posture

and muscles?

Again and again, I have witnessed how a person's thoughts and beliefs have shaped their bodies over time. Posture reveals EVERYTHING about your subconscious mind. I used to do body readings, I could tell everything about their lives, their past, and their personality just by observing their posture and how they moved and held their body.

People thought I was clairvoyant because I was spot on every time, however once you understand the MindBody connection it then becomes highly obvious. Posture reveals personality and thought patterns, because subconscious thoughts affect the muscles that shape our bodies.

What posture do you most identify with?

red light

The red-light posture is fear-based, indicating 'holding back' from life. Those with this posture tend to focus on the past. The posture is defined by an anterior tilt (pelvis tucked under), which creates a flat back with weak muscles, round shoulders, abdominal tension, tight hamstrings, and rigid legs. It's a stooped downward posture.

Perpetually fearful thoughts, cause the body to draw inwards for protection. This stops energy from flowing freely, which can cause leg injuries, bladder irritability, abdominal tension, lower back pain, tension headaches, and gynaecological problems. Those with a red-light posture also tend to block sexual expression and/or hold on to sexual feelings.

This posture typically indicates somebody who lacks confidence.

During one of my MindBody workshops, Anna realised she had a severe red-light posture. She walked slowly, with her shoulders hunched and her eyes fixed on the floor—not a confident posture.

We did a walking exercise to pinpoint her centre of gravity and correct her posture, but she felt uncomfortable when she tried to straighten her spine and 'think tall'. I asked her why she didn't feel comfortable with having a more confident upright posture.

"Because everyone will think I'm a stuck-up snob who's too big for her boots," she replied.

She was certain that's how she'd be viewed and determined

to avoid being judged as such.

"Why do you think people would think that?" I enquired.

She described in great detail "a nasty, stuck-up bitch from high school, who walked around with a pole stuck-up her backside, ordering people about and being cruel."

Anna had been bullied by this girl, and she unconsciously linked an upright posture with being stuck-up and cruel. Once Anna was aware of this mis-association, we worked on reprogramming her MindBody to believe that good posture represented health, grace, and wisdom, and she was able to walk tall again.

This is a common example of how thoughts embody us and shape our lives.

green light

The Green Light Posture (lordosis) features a postural tilt, which means the pelvis tilts backwards, the bottom jutting outwards. A person with the green light posture often has a curvature of the lower spine and is likely to have tight lower back muscles, which are usually accompanied by weak and extended abdominal muscles. The quadriceps muscles in the thighs will also tend to be tight, and the hamstrings are usually weak.

In this posture, the head is often thrown forward, causing a sore neck. This posture type is usually found in people who are open to life and think a lot about the future.

In extreme cases, the mind races ahead and the body can't keep up, creating the forward-leaning posture of an impatient, hyperactive doer who is always in a hurry. Is it any wonder they have tight, sore leg muscles?

A deeper exploration of posture and posture personality types can be found in my book *Your MindBody Journey*

What emotions are linked to health issues?
And where do they show up in the body?

Thoughts and feelings are channelled through the body as energy. However, if that flow of energy becomes blocked, for whatever reason, then that energy of unreleased thoughts and emotions manifest within the body as a physical condition.

where is your pain?

The Moving Centre

The area between the hips and the ground is known as the "Moving Centre." It includes the hips, legs, and feet—the body parts we use for locomotion.

The feet indicate how strong, stable, and grounded we are—our capacity to "stand on our own two feet."
The ankles and knees represent our resistance to or acceptance of change. Being "brought to your knees" means being forced to surrender to change.

Legs represent our direction in life, and hips, our support, stability, foundation, and security. Any issues in the Moving Centre, or messages from this part of the body, are usually linked to loss of direction or a sense of instability.

- I've got cold feet.
- I can't stand it.
- I don't have a leg to stand on.
- I need to put my foot down.
- I can't stand up for myself.

- I've lost my footing.
- S/he's under my feet.

These sayings inform the conscious mind of what's going on in the subconscious mind.

The Being Centre

The torso—chest, tummy, and spine—form the "Being Centre" of the body.
The front of the torso indicates how we "front" the world—"s/he puts up a good front."

It's the home of our self-esteem and willpower and therefore influences the way we express emotions. The chest is where feelings of love and pain are experienced, and it's where we feel that sense of aliveness. It's home to our lungs, which control our breath and our "pranayama" (a Sanskrit word to describe our life force).

The tummy is the home of the intuitive self. It's where gut feelings come from. It's where we digest not just our food, but also our life experiences. "I can't stomach it" is a phrase we might use when life gets too much. When this happens, our digestion is disrupted, and we experience tummy issues.

The back of the Being Centre includes the spine and central nervous system. It relates to core strength, willpower, and our ability to take responsibility for our thoughts and actions.

Nobody wants to be spineless or lack a backbone. The strength of the backbone indicates our capacity to support ourselves in life. The spinal network represents the strength of our support networks.

Listen for phrases like:
- I'm bending over backward.
- I'm holding back.
- S/he turned her back on me.
- You got my back up.
- Get off my back.
- I'm going backwards.
- I felt like I was stabbed in the back.

The Doing Centre

The Doing Centre includes the arms and shoulders. It connects to the torso and is a channel through which the Being Centre can express itself. The right arm represents our masculine side: being assertive, active, and giving. It's our doing energy. The left arm represents our feminine self: being passive, intuitive, and receiving. It's our Being Energy.

Arms and shoulders express needs and wants through physical action and channel our being energy into doing energy. We "shoulder" our burdens. When shoulders hunch up (like a tortoise disappearing into its shell), it indicates being overburdened.

Listen for phrases like:

- I stay at arm's length.
- Give me some elbow room.
- I can't handle it.
- S/he twisted my arm.
- I can't hold on any longer

The Control Centre

The "Control Centre" includes the head, face and neck. The neck is the channel through which the brain communicates with the rest of the body. The Control Centre mediates thoughts and feelings.

Listen for phrases like:

- It's doing my head in.
- S/he's a pain in the neck.

- I can't see a way forward
- I can't face it

The mind operates mostly in a subconscious state, and learning to become more mindful is a process of becoming awake and conscious. Mindfulness helps you to control the subconscious mind rather than the subconscious mind controlling you.

Why does the brain avoid looking at pain?

The subconscious mind naturally avoids physical and emotional pain. It's a protection we have cleverly mastered to keep us safe. When an emotional upset is experienced, the subconscious mind does everything in its power to prevent feeling it again. This subconscious programming is far more powerful than the conscious mind, and because we're largely unaware of the thoughts and beliefs that shape our lives, we're often oblivious as to why we avoid doing something.

We download the majority of this subconscious programming between the ages of 0–6, from our parents and the culture we're born into. Early experiences shape the subconscious, and we're driven by this programming until a new program or pattern replaces it.

hidden truths

Physical pain is often linked to emotional pain, and because emotional pain causes extreme stress, the subconscious mind will resist examining it at all costs. Typically, to avoid having to deal with pain, we blame it on something or someone else. However, what we resist, persists. Until it's resolved, healed, or a new pattern of health is established, the pain will continue.

Biologist and author Dr. Bruce Lipton discovered that fewer than 5% of us are born with faulty genes. This means that the vast majority of disease and illness is caused by lifestyle. And our actions, thoughts, beliefs, and stress are the component parts of lifestyle. The neural pathways in our brains are like superhighways packed with nerve cells, constantly sending instructions to the rest of the body, and once programmed to do a certain task, a certain way, we'll repeat that pattern until we're programmed to do things differently.

What happens if we chose to ignore our pain?

Ignoring pain is futile. It will intensify until it gets the attention it needs, often resulting in an accident, injury, or life crisis.

Painkillers can numb pain messages from the brain. Sometimes we choose to numb pain because we're busy and need to get on with life, and sometimes we're fearful of what we might find.

If we point-blank refuse to address pain over a long period, we can even develop a psychological numbness as a form of protection. Numbness is safe, but it suppresses and denies true spirit, light and joy and can leave us feeling dead inside. Feeling numb for an extended period indicates that a pain has yet to be faced.

Creating a life with feeling means letting go of the numb comfort-blanket and dealing with past pain. If we resist letting go of the numbness, the pain will intensify until it finds an outlet. Pain needs to be expressed openly with, anger, joy, sadness, creativity, grief, love, guilt, etc. if we are to heal.

The deeper, wiser part of us knows we crave living and feeling fully again.

it's all in the craving

Jessy came to me with constant pain in her back, knees, and shoulders. She'd had many horse-riding accidents and worked as a horse trainer and a dog groomer. So, her physical pain had obvious physical causes.

In her first session, I treated her symptoms with deep tissue massage and rehabilitation techniques. Once I started working on her body, however, it became clear there was a lot of other healing to be addressed. Her body was crying out to be noticed, loved and nurtured, but she'd never listened to it. Only after a near-fatal horse-riding accident did she stop forcing her body and seek the care she was craving.

In our second session, she was ready to look at the truth behind her pain, and it became apparent that she'd spent 50 years blocking love. Her childhood was loveless, and her mother told her repeatedly that she didn't want a girl. She was never hugged or told she was loved. Consequently, Jessy believed, from an early age, that she wasn't of value and wasn't loved. In adulthood, she attracted abusive relationships, which confirmed her belief that she wasn't worthy of love.

"When I had my daughter," she said, "I had to force myself to tell her I loved her. I never wanted to be like my mother."

Giving love didn't come naturally to her, and she even found hugging hard. Early in her life, she'd unconsciously closed her heart and erected defensive barriers to protect herself from being rejected again. She'd stopped feeling and become comfortably numb.

Jessy began to realise that she'd neglected herself just like her mother had. Her body was crying out to be loved, but love couldn't penetrate her defensive barriers. Suddenly, she understood why she'd never had close friendships or relationships. She always thought she'd been rejected but now understood that she'd been doing the rejecting all along.

When this truth came to the surface, I observed a physical softening in her as she relaxed and dropped her armour. The transformation was complete when she trusted love enough to let it in.

A few weeks later, she reported that her knee and shoulder pain had completely gone, and her back pain eased every day.

suppressed emotions create pain

If our emotions haven't been expressed and released, they'll manifest within the body as a physical condition. Emotion is energy; energy in motion (emotion) and if energy is suppressed, then it will show up somewhere else.

One of my clients, Katrina, suffered badly from indigestion. She tried everything to fix it: fasting, dieting, homeopathy, kinesiology, massage, herbal remedies, digestive enzymes, and even aloe vera. No matter what she tried or what she ate, she still had indigestion day and night.

I asked her what she "couldn't stomach" and she shared the story of an ongoing family upset. She'd been betrayed by a couple of family members and felt sad that she couldn't trust the people she loved the most. It was "eating away'" at her.

I gave her body an energy healing, and when I reached her stomach, I felt an energy void and the overwhelming pain of her feelings of betrayal. Energetically, she'd been "stabbed in the back." She confirmed that is exactly what she felt and that is exactly what had happened to her. We reclaimed her energy and I helped her to let go and forgive the people who were "eating away at her insides."

The next day, she phoned me, full of joy.
"I can't believe that my indigestion has completely disappeared. I can't thank you enough.

"This is why I love my work!

feel to heal

Have you ever fought back tears because it's an inappropriate time and place to cry like a baby? Think about the inner control needed to hold back energy of that magnitude. Where does it go?

We bind it up tightly in the physical body where it clogs our energy channels. And, as we know, the energy of our suppressed emotions will find a way to communicate through physical signs and symptoms. Many chronic illnesses have unleashed tears at their root.

Let's be honest, when was the last time you had a jolly good cry? Not a little whimper, or a few leaky tears, but a good hearty howl that came from deep within. Probably not for a long time.

How many times have you felt like chucking a tantrum like a child, but instead swallowed your
emotions and moved on? If you were told as a child not to cry, to pull yourself together and not make a scene, then this programming may still be running your emotional life.

To stop physical pain, emotional pain needs to be released first. Our tears help us heal. They unleash suppressed emotions and release heavy burdens, deeply clearing channels as they flow. Even the sound of a cry sends healing vibrations to the root of the pain.

Feeling safe enough to express emotion is unfortunately rare. Often, we don't fully vent our emotions because we don't trust them, or fear being judged for them. Sitting with a therapist or close friend who doesn't try to fix, resolve, or stop the tears, but instead witnesses and validates them, is to receive a loving gift.

To release suppressed tears, you might ask yourself these types of questions:

- Do I have pain that is patiently waiting to be expressed?
- What hurts and heartaches still weigh heavily on my heart?
- How does my little inner child need to feel loved and cherished?
- Am I carrying pain and suffering for others?

Regardless of what you've been told, regardless of what you think, regardless of what anyone else thinks, YOUR FEELINGS MATTER.

Jakkie, tell us a story about healing emotional trauma presented as pain.

Daisy came to see me for energy healing that she hoped would help her aches and pains. I suspected there was something deeper going on and so I started by asking her how she felt.

She complained of a tight knot in her tummy that caused her constant pain. She'd always been slim but had developed fat around her belly that she couldn't shift, despite exercise and diet. Her 5-year-old daughter was experiencing outbursts of rage that seemed to come from nowhere. She'd compensated with assurances of love, but the rage continued.

Her mother and sister-in-law had turned against her and were manipulating her husband into not liking her. She'd lost friends in the past to this kind of betrayal.

"It sounds like this feeling of betrayal and abuse is common in your life. Have you experienced abuse before?" I pushed, hoping she'd reveal more.

She told me that she'd been bullied at school and beaten every day by her schoolmates. This bullying had started when she was five—her daughter's age. As she was telling me her story, we could hear a child crying uncontrollably, shouting and screaming outside in the street. The child's rage was no coincidence!

"Do you hear that rage?" I asked. "It's the rage you never expressed when you were a child and it's the rage you need to feel now." She burst into tears and told me she'd been raped on three separate occasions in her teenage years.

Her actions and reactions throughout her life came from

feeling deeply undervalued and unloved and resulted in abusive relationships and dramas with her friends. The belief that she wasn't of value and not loved was cemented into her subconscious the first time she was bullied.

So, we worked on reprogramming this subconscious belief about herself by honouring her suppressed rage at her abusers and truly acknowledging that she didn't deserve that treatment at such a young age. She voiced her anger at what had happened to her, as if it was happening anew. The knot in her stomach, which for many years had bound her rage, travelled up to her heart so that she could feel her sadness. "I can feel the knot in my stomach dissolving. I feel so light!" she said.

The next stage of the healing process was to rewire the belief that she was not loved, and she started by loving the little girl who was abused.

As part of this journey, she realised she was a "people pleaser". She went out of her way to please those around her because she wanted to feel valued and loved. But because she believed she gave more love than she received, a vicious cycle of overpleasing and disappointment developed.

This confirmed her belief that she wasn't loved.

These feelings fuelled the rage that she wasn't able to express in her childhood. And because she was ashamed of her rage, she kept it locked in her tummy.

back on track

We devised a plan: every time her daughter expressed rage, she would feel it as her own. Instead of trying to pacify her daughter, Daisy let her express the rage she never could.

She then started looking for evidence in her life where she was loved, without overpleasing to receive it. This was the start of her self-love journey.

The false belief that she wasn't loved and that she deserved abuse was reprogrammed with the belief that she deserved unconditional love. She replaced the rage in her belly with self-empowerment and self-love.

She lost her innocence, purity, love, and trust at the age of five, so we called the lost parts back, and bit by bit, we brought her broken pieces back together.

The knot in her tummy is no longer there, and the fat around her belly, which she'd built up to protect herself, naturally dissolved. But the biggest result is her child, who no longer cries with rage.

Jakkie, tell us a story about healing physical pain.

Belinda came to see me because of constant lower back pain. The pain stemmed back to a car accident when she was a teenager—her mother and she had collided with one another on impact. They were both given the all-clear, but Belinda developed pain in her lower back a few months later. Over the next 20 years, she saw every kind of specialist, but no one could diagnose what was wrong with her spine.

"What does the pain feel like?" I asked.

"A constant thorn in my side! I feel split in half most of the time. And, I'm sick and tired of feeling pain."

Her mother had drug problems, and their relationship was strained. When she was a little girl, her mother kidnapped her while she was in the care of her father. The police found them; her father won custody and her mum was denied access.

"Most of the time, I felt split between my parents. I felt constantly guilty about my mum," she said.

Belinda became an overprotective mother of three. She felt the weight of responsibility for her children's safety and moved houses often because of an irrational fear that her mother would find her and try to take the children.

She'd lost her trust in people and tried to control everything, building a life structured to keep her children safe. It was exhausting for her. She felt the pain of loss and separation so deeply that it had become a physical "thorn in her side."

We worked on rewiring her belief that "bad things were going to happen." I encouraged her to listen to her pain instead of constantly blocking it out. It had to be heard, to be healed. This helped her let go of her need to control everyone and everything around her. Two weeks later, she reported that she felt like a new woman—free and light.

"I no longer feel like I have a thorn in my side. I love my kids and I'm not scared that bad things will happen to them. And oh my god, the best part is that my mum and I are becoming friends. I'm so happy!

the missing pieces

It takes true courage to dig deep and uncover the suffering behind physical dis-ease and pain, but once acknowledged, expressed, and released, life flourishes. Facing deep issues relieves the soul, and can even be a surprisingly fun and joyous process.

People's pain patterns are like a complex jigsaw puzzle. Once the pieces are put into place, wholeness and completion emerge, and a beautiful scene appears.

Can we feel sympathetic pain?

Yes, absolutely! One of my clients took on the pain of her child to prevent her child from suffering. Some men experience Couvade, or "sympathetic pregnancy", and feel the symptoms of pregnancy and the pain of childbirth with their partners. Subconsciously, they would rather share the pain than see a loved one suffer.

Veterinarians have even witnessed pets absorbing patterns of pain and/or the emotions of their owners. When a friend's mother's dog died of a rare condition, she bought another dog, which then died of the same rare condition. The theory behind this "coincidence" was that the pets absorbed the emotional pain of their owner, preventing the owner from getting sick—now that's unconditional love!

Can our pain be inherited from our ancestors?

Yes. Sometimes the pain we experience isn't even our own. Pain can be inherited from previous generations. It's not necessarily passed down by a genetic mutation or in the DNA from the mother or father, but rather it's inherited as an energetic cellular memory code in our genes. It can stay dormant or be triggered when something significant happens in our lives.

Inherited pain may be activated when we experience the same emotion that the ancestor linked to the original pain. This turns on the inherited cellular memory and the physical pain that your ancestors experienced. If you have family members with similar aches and pains to yours, then it's an indication that the issues may be inherited.

Our thoughts and beliefs are also passed down from generation to generation. We take on board the beliefs of our family and the culture we're born into and accept these beliefs as gospel truth. Ask yourself these types of questions about your subconscious beliefs to find out whether you're carrying ancestral pain:

- Do I believe I have a family curse?
- Do I believe I was born into a sick or unhealthy family?
- Do I believe it's only a matter of time before I catch the latest virus?
- Do I believe my immune system is weak?
- Am I prone to sickness and disease because of the toxins in my food or my environment?

It's only when we become aware of our beliefs that we can question them and change them.

If you believe you have inherited your pain, then you can choose to stop the pattern of pain now.

cut the chain

- Acknowledge that the pain isn't yours.
- Forgive your ancestor or family member for passing it on to you.

- Stop the pattern of pain by choosing a different set of beliefs about your health.

- Choose an affirmation or mantra to rewire your health belief, something like, 'My body is constantly healthy and full of energy.' Choose one that feels right for you, then repeat the words as often as you remember. The key is to believe it! Remember the body doesn't know the difference between fantasy or reality, it just responds to thought.

- Visualise every cell in your body being healthy and full of life. You can imagine this as a crystal-clear waterfall, cascading down through the top of your head and into every cell of your body, washing away all impurities with it. Do this every day until you feel a positive shift in your health.

Can pain be bought into this life from a previous life?

Humans have long believed that the soul is eternal, and many believe in reincarnation theory, which states that each of us has had multiple lives in multiple dimensions and that data about previous lives is stored in cellular memory.

Even though personally I believe in this theory, I'm cautious about suggesting a person's repeated pain is because of a past life issue. However, I have gone there with a few of my clients who have been open this concept.

I'd given Jill's arm a few treatments and wasn't getting results, so I began to suspect there was something deeper going on.

"Jill," I asked, "what's the feeling behind the pain?"
"It feels shattered and disconnected," she said.

We studied the pain together for a short while. Suddenly, she grabbed my arm and looked at me with wide eyes.
"You'll never believe this!"

"Try me!" I said.

Years ago, she'd had past life regression therapy, and it dawned on her that in each of her five past lives, she'd damaged her left arm. The most traumatic was during the Battle of Hastings in 1066, when her arm was chopped off. Past life memories can be dubious because the subconscious mind often throws up what it wants to believe. I kept an open mind and agreed to do a healing on her arm.

Jill's body shook throughout the treatment. She saw images of a jigsaw being put back together and streams of liquid pouring into her head and down through her body like a network of rivers. I saw something similar during the healing, but mine was like a matrix of lines all reconnecting again.

The next day, Jill sent me the following message:

"Last night I felt strange but drank lots of water and went to bed. I woke at 2 am. I was wide awake and felt full of energy. I couldn't get back to sleep! I can't believe it, but my shoulder pain has completely gone! And my energy levels are high, despite the lack of sleep".

heading back

Another time, a client came to see me about constant headaches. He'd tried various diets, meditation, and drugs; he'd had a brain scan and seen various specialists, but no one could find the cause of his constant headache.

Before his first session, I tuned into his energy to get a sense of what he needed. In a flash, I saw a vivid image of him in mediaeval times, wearing an executioner's mask and holding an axe. Shocked, I allowed the scene to unfold and saw him beheading people.

I refrained from blurting out, "I know what's wrong with you! You were an axe-wielding executioner in a previous life, and your headaches are probably your Karma!" Instead, I probed gently.

He told me that he felt constant guilt, sought punishment, and blamed himself for everything. He felt guilty for not being able to work and provide for his family. He felt guilty that he couldn't play with his kids because of his headaches. He felt guilty for being a burden to his wife.

He felt so guilty that he'd started to self-harm to punish himself. It didn't matter if the past life vision I had seen was true or not, his guilt needed to be healed at a cellular level. I suggested he see a psychotherapist or a counsellor, but he didn't believe it was a psychological issue. He refused point-blank to look deeper to resolve old patterns of pain. I wasn't surprised.

He has no idea what I saw—I never told him. When he's ready to let go of his guilt and ready to forgive himself, he can start to heal.

What is the process you use to help people heal their pain?

The first step for healing, is to find and release the psycho-emotional root cause attached to the physical pain.

The second stage of the process is to clear and rewire the body and mind so that the pain pattern isn't repeated. The brain is wired to feel emotional pain every time we think of physical pain. This keeps the emotional pain and physical pain locked together in a looping pattern. The loop can be broken by consciously replacing the negative image and associated emotion with a positive emotion.

In some cases, there's no emotional pain attached to the physical pain, so we use techniques to send signals to the body to become well, like a placebo.

However, in my experience, all humans have some degree of psycho-emotional pain stored in their bodies, whether they admit it or not. Staying positive is a great tool, but it can mask or bypass deep wounds, keeping us stuck in a pattern of pain. When we're continually triggered emotionally, it's a clear indication that there's still emotional pain stuck in the body.

If the emotional pain has not been confronted and healed, the emotional triggers will often get worse, and down the track it's likely to manifest in the body as an ache, pain, or disease.

To prevent the physical manifestation of unreleased emotional pain, we must take responsibility for our triggers and emotional pains. It's easy to ignore triggers or blame others for them, but when we do this, we remain locked in a pattern of pain—our own personal hell.

Once you're ready to truly heal, then your transformation can begin. Over many years, I've had the honour of helping hundreds of people transform their pain into freedom.
I won't heal you, YOU heal you!

you can heal yourself

Every discovery about a clients subconscious patterning and wounding comes from within them. My job is to help uncover what's already hidden inside of that person. I then facilitate the reprogramming by giving them the right tools, methods, and actions to activate their own healing process. All of us already have our unique medicine inside of us, we just need to know how to activate it.

Every person's path is unique, and your journey has brought you to here for a reason.

This is where your personal transformation begins.

Why is it necessary for us to have pain before we can experience our power?

It isn't necessary to experience pain to gain self-empowerment. But if we lack self-worth, constantly feel fear, are unhappy, unhealthy or have trauma trapped in our body, pain is the jolt we need to nudge us into healing. We sometimes need to experience the pain of our darkness to enable us to discover our true powerful light. Increasing pain and suffering is our dark night of the soul where we have the option to go one of two ways; we can go further down a path of pain and suffering to our demise, or we can delve deep, find our inner strength, and rise towards health and happiness. That is our power.

It is also a journey of death and rebirth, from an old way of being to a new way of being.

Sometimes big things must happen to us, to crack us open, to break us down completely for us to be rebuilt again. This is sometimes what needs to happen to transform us completely from one state into another, just like the butterfly. It is a caterpillar first, which must then turn into a pulpy mushy mess which enables it to turn into a completely different beautiful species. That is transformation.

When our pain becomes so intense and we hit rock bottom, we are pushed into a raw, dark place where we experience extreme vulnerability. It brings up a lot of fear, doubt, helplessness and often uncovers old childhood wounds (the messy mush). But if we embrace the experience and surrender ourselves completely to it, rather than resist it, or get stuck in it, then the floodgate of emotions can rise and finally the heaviness and all that's attached to it, gets released. When we do this, we release not just the present pains and suffering, but all the pains of the past too. This is a form of purging, of emptying, of releasing the old.

Then at some point we rise back up, just like a buoy that has been submerged under the water. We rise with such momentum that we become lighter, freer, stronger, more courageous, leading us into being more compassionate and open hearted. Just like the butterfly, we have transformed into a beautiful new being. We become reborn.

Jakkie, can you give an example of your own journey transforming your pain into power?

Yes, I have many, where do I begin?!

On a physical level I have healed many recurring pain patterns; from eating disorders, perpetual teeth problems, constant kidney infections, knee arthritis, to so many repeated accidents and injuries (especially to my right leg).

On an emotional level I have healed a lot of my fears and traumas by facing them head on. I did most of this unconsciously the long way, this was before I learnt that I didn't have to go through such extremes to heal!

Here are some of them:

I was very shy as a child; I had no confidence and could barely speak a word to anyone. But I faced my shyness and lack of confidence and have since performed on stage in front of hundreds of people.

I have been humiliated and sacked from many jobs. I had a belief I was useless and a failure and became very depressed and unmotivated. It took a while, but I finally found my self worth and a belief in myself which helped me to climb back up. I was then appointed as creative manager for a well-known London design agency, and finally head hunted by a leading natural health magazine and was appointed their art director.

I was trampled on and almost killed by a herd of angry cows and yet I can now walk into a field of cows with no hesitation.

I've had my heart broken again and again, and I've put the pieces back together again and again, each time in a slightly better order.

I had a fear of heights, but I jumped out of a plane and skydived at 14,000 feet. I also bungee jumped from a crane onto concrete. I now LOVE heights!

I stood my ground when I was almost sold as a slave in Pakistan (don't ask!).

I was lost for a day and night in a remote Australian rainforest, but I stepped into my resourcefulness, used my intuition, and found my way back out.

One day on a deserted beach, I was attacked at gunpoint by

a masked man who tried to rape me. Somehow, I found the strength to fight him off, even though the gun was loaded. After a lot of therapy, I realised it was the catalyst for confronting and healing my fear of intimacy and mistrust of men. This put an end to my repeated relationship disasters, and I finally found my soul mate.

I've had to face my fears, and overcome struggle so many times in my life, but the most emotionally painful experience I've ever had to do, is to help my darling mum die. This was something I didn't think I would ever recover from.

Jakkie, can you share this painful story and how you managed to find your strength?

Ok, so just after Covid lockdown in 2022, I made the choice to leave my home in Australia, my partner, my business to fly back to the UK to care for my elderly mum who was struggling to live on her own. I managed to get her properly diagnosed with Alzheimer's and went about trying to get her the help and support she needed. I struggled caring for her as she resisted her condition and wouldn't let go of her old life, especially her pride. She kept saying she didn't want to continue to live if she was going to end up going mad!

Helping her to accept her 'new normal' was one challenge, but what I wasn't banking on was for her to fulfil her wish by having two separate brain haemorrhages, and then watching her slowly and painfully die.

The worst part was not being able to get her the help she needed, because all the health professionals kept saying her symptoms were just her increasing Alzheimer's and there was nothing anyone could do. It wasn't until I finally managed to get her hospitalised that it was clear that her brain damage was caused by the undiagnosed haemorrhages. If she had been properly diagnosed earlier, she would've lived.

I stayed by her hospital bedside, and I tried to be so brave and strong for her while I witnessed the constant terror in her eyes. I kept whispering in her ear that it was OK to let go of her life, she was safe, that there was nothing to fear, and that love was waiting for her on the other side, ready to greet her with open arms.

Ten days later, she finally gave up the fight and made the transition.

I had encouraged her to die, but what I didn't take into consideration, was how I'd feel once she'd gone. I'd been so strong for her and once she'd left, I crashed into a state of absolute despair. All that strength I had shown her had left me, and instead it was replaced with such deep sadness, grief, and loss that I didn't think I'd survive another day with the pain. Now I understand the meaning, 'being weighed down with grief' because I felt 20 pounds heavier. The weight in my heart felt suffocating, like I was deep sea diving without oxygen.

This was my dark night of the soul.

All I wanted to do was crawl into a hole and hide away, but I couldn't because there were all the official things to sort out. It all got way too much for me and I was starting to breakdown.

However somewhere from deep within me I pulled up more strength, and with my broken heart, I managed to organise my mum's funeral, commission stones and plaques for 3 memorials, I sorted out all the official documents, sold her car, cleared out all her belongings from the house, cleared out my own lifetime of belongings stored in her loft, got the house ready to sell - all while supporting my sister who had mental health issues.

And then I got COVID, just before I was due to fly back to Australia.

This hit me hard, really hard, I could barely move from my bed from one day to the next, and I was completely alone. There was no one to rescue me, to take care of me or nurture me, not even the health system could help me, because at the time it was overrun with other Covid patients. The only person that could help me was me.

I was in and out of consciousness for what felt like months, but it was only weeks. I had to dig deep and trust this too shall pass, that this time in bed was just what I needed to gain strength. I gave myself the love and nurture I needed and finally I got physically well enough to get on a plane.

It was a monumental moment saying goodbye to my family home, the memories, my roots, and closing the door to my past for the last time. I took a deep breath and headed to the airport to take me back to Australia.

Only a few days after I landed, when I thought things can now only get better, they didn't! I was then the subject of an extremely cruel betrayal by a close family member that cut so deep it felt like I was being crucified.

What I was being accused of by this person, and the abuse that was being projected onto me was pure emotional torture, because I knew it wasn't true. It was their own pain and suffering being projected onto me. I knew that when someone is reluctant to look within themselves and take responsibility for their own pain, wounds, and darkness, they will project their blind spots onto other people, blaming others for their suffering, keeping themselves locked into their own delusional pattern of pain. I knew this was what was happening to me, but it didn't make the betrayal any easier to accept at that point.

My body couldn't take any more emotional pain, so I slumped back into another dark night of the soul.
There was no way my body could sustain any more stress and pain, something had to shift.

I had to make a choice. Do I let this pain destroy me or can I somehow rise above it?
Do I resist this pain, or do I let go and surrender even more?

Do I respond in fear to it, or do respond in love to it?

Do I allow all this pain and suffering to become my story, or do I see it as one of life's challenges, roll up my sleeves and get on with it?

Do I close my heart and become hardened by all the adversity, or do I see it as an opportunity to open my heart wider?

Do I choose to become a victim of my life and my experiences, or do I become a victor over them?

Do I choose to hate the pain and suffering, or do I choose to give them love?

I chose love.

Once I surrendered and expressed ALL my pain, and had processed and accepted all that had happened, I was then able to open my heart and heal. I forgave myself and others. My love shone the light on the pain and suffering and helped me to see the truth.

I finally saw the gift I had gained from it all.

This experience took me to a whole new level of love, for myself, and for others, which amplified other people's love back to me in such a profound way.

Because behind every pain we experience, there is also our power.

Behind every adversity lies our gift. We just need to step out of the story of the pain and suffering for us to see it.

When we experience the dark night of the soul, or a deep grief for something or someone we have lost, we will never be the same again. This is a certainty. Because we don't just grieve the person or thing we have lost, we grieve the person we *were* before we experienced the loss. However, birth and death is natural. It is NORMAL for things to die, but our resistance towards accepting our loss is why we feel so much pain and suffering.

By facing my own personal darkness and pain, I found my light. I learnt that I didn't have to get stuck in endless pain patterns, all I needed was a willingness to look deeper, to understand the truth behind my pain, and to allow my pain to guide me back to a place of love and vitality.

Now I'm so fine tuned to my body, my senses, my intuition, my inner compass, that pain is no longer the nudge in my life to get back on the right track. And because I am now free from my own repeating patterns of pain and learnt the tools to rise above life's painful challenges, I have gained the gift of helping others to transform their own pain into their power.

Jakkie, your healing methods are very unique, how do people find you?

It still astounds me how often a stranger openly shares their pain and emotional story with me.

the right time and place

My favourite example was when a jolly cheeky chap arrived too early to install my internet. Seeing that I was in a session with a client, he offered to come back in an hour.

As he connected our internet service, he asked about my work. When I told him I was a therapist and healer, he told me about all his aches and pains, which people often do.

His pain sometimes made getting out of bed difficult, and this wasn't helped by the depression he'd suffered since his brother's death. His depression was so bad that his wife left him and took his 10-year-old son with her.

He felt that his bad luck was unfair. 'I'm a happy, kind person, so why do I get such bad luck?' He inquired. I could see that his cheeky jokes were a coping mechanism, and he admitted that inside he was sad. He'd contemplated suicide but resisted because of his son. He was ready to heal, and I knew he'd been sent to me because he was ready.

On another occasion, I was holidaying with my partner in north Queensland. We were staying in a remote town and coincidentally bumped into a couple my partner knew. We met up for a meal that evening.

While the men talked sports, we women shared stories. She told me about her mum, who'd died of cancer a few years prior. She was petrified of getting cancer herself. She also told me about her abusive ex-partner and her father's abuse of her mother. I noted the inter-generational pattern of abuse and shared a little about the work I do. She took away my book to read.

A year later, we coincidently bumped into each other again—this time on the other side of the country.

"Your book changed my life," she said.

I was delighted to see her and eager to hear her story. We sat in a café, and she told me that after our previous meeting, she'd embarked on a profound healing journey. She released the destructive subconscious patterns that had been passed down from previous generations.

"I'm no longer frightened of cancer," she said.

Knowing the subconscious as I do, I smiled and thought to myself, I doubt cancer will be an issue for you or your family ever again.

Another time, I was running three months of workshops in Western Australia, and my partner and I decided to try housesitting while we were there. I got a call from a woman keen on utilising our services.

During our conversation, she told me of her health conditions and her trouble with her father. I didn't want my visit to her home to turn into a therapy session, so I suggested she come to the workshop I was running that weekend in Perth. She did, and it changed the course of her life.

The complex orchestration of events involved in someone arriving at my door transcends serendipity. I've learned to trust that when it happens, the person has arrived in my life because they're ready. And because you are reading this, I suspect you are ready now too.

How can the knowledge of the MindBody connection help me and my life?

your magic

Once the MindBody connection is fully understood, you'll realise that you've been secretly housing a magical storehouse of power.

The MindBody connection isn't just a method of healing. It can be used to:

- reduce stress;
- send more blood to the muscles to increase strength;
- discover whether or not certain foods are healthy for you;
- even to find lost objects; or
- to manifest your heart's desire.

Manifesting my heart's desire is my favourite use of the MindBody connection.

Jakkie, how did you first become aware of the power of manifestation?

I first became conscious of the law of manifestation (sometimes called the law of attraction) when I emigrated to Australia from the UK. I lived in Sydney but had a yearning to explore the rainforests of Queensland. Unfortunately, I had limited time and money, so taking a month off to go trekking on my own seemed unlikely. Nevertheless, the desire to explore the North had a hold on me.

During a meditation, with feelings of pure joy in my heart, I pictured myself in the rainforests of Queensland and on deserted beaches picking coconuts up off the ground. It felt so real in my mind that I was quite disappointed when I found myself back on my sofa in my city apartment.

"I WILL go to Queensland when the time is right," I assured myself.

A few months later, a window opened when some commitments came to an end. However, my funds were still insufficient to finance a month off work, and I thought I'd have to put my dream on hold again.

"Remember your power. Remember, anything is possible," prompted my inner voice.

Once again, I meditated on my perfect Queensland trip, imagining how it looked and felt. That evening, I had dinner with friends. My friend, Jim, told me that he was going to Brisbane the following week to do some promotional filming for a new product. He needed a presenter for the film, and the person he was going to use had other commitments.

"Oh Jakkie, you could do that. You used to do acting, didn't you?" my cherished friend Jess interjected.

"Well, yes... yes, I did, but..."

"Great!" said Jim. "Are you free next week for a rainforest shoot in Queensland? I'll cover flights, accommodation and pay for your time, of course."

"I'm sure I can rearrange a few things and make it work," I said, trying not to jump up on my seat and punch the air with my fist with a big fat "YES!"

The following week, I was in Queensland. We did a two-day shoot and, with cash in my pocket, I spent the rest of the month exploring the rainforest and picking coconuts up off the beach.

take a quantum leap of faith

Everything on this planet is energy and space, even though all the physical things around us appear to be solid. Every human on planet Earth is made up of millions and millions of atoms which all are 99.999% empty space. If you were to remove all the empty space contained in every atom in every person on planet earth and compress us all together, then the overall volume of our particles would be smaller than a sugar cube!

Therefore, we are pure energy vibrating at a certain frequency, and we are constantly affected by other energies and frequencies around us.

We can just about get our heads around that because we know there are energies we can't see like electricity, radio waves, microwaves, inferred, ultraviolet, and they all hold power. However, quantum physics takes our understanding of energy to a whole new complicated level! But by understanding how we operate on a quantum level, we will start to understand how, as energy beings, we create our own reality.

Quantum scientists have discovered that a quantum of light, or photon, will behave like a particle or a wave depending on how they measure it—the photon is a wave or a particle depending on what you expect to happen!

Humans are the same. We will become whatever we expect to be. Our beliefs shape and our lives.

How can we be aware of our unique energy?

First practise sensing your energy by rubbing your hands together and feel the tingling static between your hands and fingers. This is your energy. Place your hands on your legs and feel the energy increase where they connect. Close your eyes and notice the energy tingling throughout your body.

Direct the energy down to your feet with slow, deep breaths. Push the energy down with your breath. This is a good way to feel grounded. Some people even feel their bowels start to move if the energy has stimulated that part of the body.

Next, direct your energy upward by focusing your attention above your head. You're taking your energy out of your physical body and into the etheric body. This is the energy field around your body—your "personal space". When your energy exits through the top of your head, you might feel a little dizzy or lightheaded. To centre yourself again, bring your attention into your tummy and be aware of your breath.

As you practise using your thoughts and feelings to direct your energy, you'll become better equipped to change your energy when you feel out of sorts. Spending time focused inwardly will give you a fresh perspective on the outward world, and you'll be less likely to be pulled into life's dramas.

How can we use our energy to shift pain?

Pain is energy. Too much energy manifests in the body as inflammation and stimulation, and too little energy manifests as depletion and stagnation. Resistance creates friction. Energy requires oxygen for fuel, and we oxygenate our blood when we breathe. So, one of the most effective ways to heal and restore the body is to move.

When we move, we bring fresh, oxygenated blood to receptor sites in the lymphatic system, which aids healing.

Doing some form of exercise or practice every day will help the body oxygenate, recharge, reset and heal.

Instead of finding an exercise routine or practice that someone else has designed, find your own unique way to move your body. Remember, your body knows how to heal itself, so it's important to take a moment to feel into your body and let it tell you how it wants to move. It might need slow, gentle stretches, or it might need to jump about like a mad person. How does your body want to move? There is no right or wrong. Learn to use your intuition and allow your body to choose.

If it's painful to move, then be honest with yourself; is fear stopping you from leaning into the pain? If so, what's behind the fear? Have you forgotten to trust your body? Are you frightened of what might happen if you do? Remember, pain is the body's cry for attention. It wants to be moved, to be challenged, to be woken up, to be worked on. Trust that the energy knows where to flow to release stuck energy.

How can we move our energy to shift pain?

There are two ways energy can move: outward (releasing, doing, surrendering) or inward (nourishing, being, nurturing).

To move stuck energy outward, you might try: dancing, shouting, running, jumping, flicking, and exhaling while moving your arms outwards with the intention of moving stuck energy out of your body.

To bring energy back into the body, you might try: meditation, massage, hugs, thinking loving thoughts about yourself, eating nourishing food, slow mindful walks in nature, exhaling while moving your arms inwards with the intention of bringing new energy into your body.

the bigger picture

Energy channels flow in and out of the body via our chakras and meridians. These channels are directly connected to our aura (an energy field around the body) and our aura is connected to the universal energy (all energy). Science is starting to understand that universal energy is an intelligent energy and that we're not separate from it, but rather we ARE the universal energy.

Every minute of every day, you unconsciously change the energetic frequency of your body with your thoughts, feelings, and intentions. Energy attracts like energy—joy attract joy. So, with your body set at the correct energy frequency, you can manifest whatever you like.

This doesn't just work on an individual level. Our thoughts, feelings, and intentions feed into the universal energy. If we collectively think and feel "peace and love," together we can manifest global change.

If we look at pandemics from a quantum perspective, they may represent the negative energy of unhealed collective pain patterns. If we collectively heal a pain pattern, we don't just heal ourselves, we can also help to heal the planet. This is how powerful we are.

Although I'm still an amateur, I've learned how to align my frequency with the deep wisdom of universal energy. I've developed this through yoga, meditation, healing, and being an open conduit of information for others. Sometimes the information I receive is pure magic.

mindbody magic

A while ago, I found out the exact time of my birth by tapping into my MindBody wisdom. I needed to know the exact second that I took my first breath for a project I was involved in. My mum was too busy birthing me at the time to take notes, so she couldn't supply me with an accurate answer, so I booked in to see a professional kinesiologist.

The kinesiologist asked my body a series of questions, and my body responded with Yes/No answers. The interesting part was that she didn't ask the questions out loud to me but telepathically to my body. My ears didn't hear her, but my body did, and I gave her a definite answer to the exact second of my birth.

Years later, I tracked down the midwife's documents and confirmed the exact moment of my birth, and it was indeed the same answer as the kinesiologist had given me.

You can use this Yes/No response method yourself. Stand with your feet on the floor and then ask your body to show you a "Yes" response. The body will lean forward, backward, or to one side. Then ask your body what a "No" response looks like. Once your Yes/No response has been established, then you can ask the body anything.

Dowsing is another good way to find personal or universal answers. Dowsing is a method of divining using rods or a pendulum. I use this method to find items that I've lost, handy I can tell you, especially when I lose the car keys! I also use dowsing when I'm unclear about my direction in life or a choice I need to make.

By learning how to master my mind, my emotions and my energy system, over time I've managed to not only heal my body but also manifest many things into my life. These include the perfect work, the ideal house, just the right amount of money, my soul mate and so much more.

If you would like to learn more about how to harness your magic and manifest the life you crave, then I highly recommend the *MindBody Magic Online Course.*

How can I develop my MindBody Connection and heal my life?

I love the famous Henry Ford quote: "Whether you think you can, or whether you think you can't—you're right." Remember the law of quantum? Matter will act like a wave or particle depending on how we expect it to behave. Therefore, our expectations will become our experience.

If you don't believe it's possible to have what you want, then you'll never have what you want. The key to creating the life you desire is the unwavering BELIEF that you'll have it. Because of the MindBody connection, if the mind believes that great health is inevitable, then the body will respond to that belief with great health.

Healthy thoughts create a healthy body because affirmation is powerful. If you think and honestly feel the absolute truth of the following statements: "my body knows how to heal," "my body is healthy" or "I'm in perfect health," your body will start to produce the right healing chemicals to confirm that belief.

Meditation, hypnosis, mindfulness, NLP, EFT, RTT, and Theta are just a few of the many practises that can help rewire the subconscious mind.

How can I learn to turn off the program of my pain?

Once you disassociate yourself from your thoughts, your body, your identity and your pain, and instead identify with your higher self, the possibilities are limitless.

Health and happiness are your natural state; you just need to uninstall the program that blocks them.

You can use your powerful mind to turn off your pain. There are many methods and mind techniques I use to help people to do this.

Jakkie, can you recommend any tips to help strengthen our MindBody connection?

Absolutely! There's lots you can do. Firstly, keep practising sensing and moving your energy which we covered earlier.

Here are some tools to help you strengthen your inner world and regain your power.

sharpen your senses

It's also helpful (and enjoyable) to become more aware of your 5 senses:

When you eat, be aware of the food in your mouth instead of mindlessly chewing. Avoid watching tv, talking or looking at your phone while eating, instead enjoy every sensation in your mouth and observe the delicious flavours of your food. Feel the breeze against your skin when you're outside. Be aware of your nostrils and how they take in air.

Spend five minutes a day tuning in to and identifying the various sounds you can hear around you. Take the time to really see the vision in front of you. Notice all the different colours, shapes, sizes, and expressions of form.

lots of laughs

Laughter is a powerful medicine that strengthens the immune system. A good belly laugh flushes the body with good hormones that clean and rebalance your mind and body. Winners are grinners!

Norman Cousins had a severe and life-threatening disease of the connective tissue called degenerative collagen illness. He was hospitalised in with severe pain, high fever and near-paralysis of the legs, neck and back. The key to his recovery, he said, was a powerful drug called laughter.

Flat on his back in a New York hospital, Cousins persuaded the nurses to show him "Candid Camera" reruns and old Marx Brothers movies.

He was cured within 6 months.

listen to yourself

Learn to listen to what your body needs. If you have an accident, injury, or just feel a little 'off', ask your body what it wants from you. What does it need? What do YOU need? Answers will come if you are open to receiving the truth instead of being resistant to what might be revealed. Keep asking your pain what it wants.

Ask your body what it needs to help you release your pain. It might want to scream and shout. It might want lots of care and nurture. You might want to switch your focus from your pain by doing something that brings you joy. You might want to watch comedy movies back-to-back! Whatever your body needs, give it to it.

Listen to your intuition to find a practise that gets you out of your head and connects you with your body and your energy. It might be yoga, meditation, tai-chi, dance, massage, singing, walking, running, swimming, gardening, sex, breathwork, baths, anything where your focus is on your body and not in your head thinking about what you're going to have for dinner that evening.

Tune into what your body needs as opposed to what others believe you need.

live in the moment

By living moment by moment, you'll be more aware of your MindBody connection working for you. If you live in your head, thinking of the past or future, then you'll miss the magic happening right NOW.

It takes constant practice to keep bringing yourself into the present moment, but once you master it, you'll realise how much of your life has been spent in your head, instead of your heart, where your gold lies.

heart v head

Learn to follow your intuition and your heart instead of always listening to your head. Your first reaction is your gut, but the rational mind loves to take over and introduce doubt. Learn to know the difference.

Your deepest inner knowing seeks your fullest life. Don't let your rational mind make you a slave to other people's lives, or an unfulfilled life because it feels safe. Nothing will change unless you change.

If you feel something is "missing" from your life, discontentment will build. It's not selfish to follow your heart; it's vitally important that you do. If you're not happy, nobody around you will be either!

watch your words

Word are spells, that's why they call it spelling! Words are energy, and energy affects energy. Therefore, it's vital to be aware of what you think and say because what you think and say will manifest! Try saying "I CAN" instead of "I CAN'T" and watch how your life changes.

Just by Repeating the words 'I am the master of my mind and body'. You set into motion your power over it.

Whatever affirmation you choose for yourself, say it out loud as often as you can, with true conviction, sincere devotion, speak from your soul and recognise the truth of who you are, which is love, health, happiness.

Do not be surprised if you experience overwhelming emotional states while you activate this power. When you perform it with complete surrender and conviction of your true self, it harnesses the power of transformation.

attitude of gratitude

Self-love and gratitude will fast track you to health and happiness.

As corny as this sounds, it's the key to living a healthy, happy life. Like attracts like, so LOVE will attract more LOVE. Gratitude will attract more things to feel grateful about. If you're riddled with self-loathing, have low self-esteem, constantly undervalue yourself, or put yourself down, you'll attract circumstances and people that will confirm this belief.

Open your heart and BE the LOVE that you crave.

BE the LOVE that you truly are.

set your intention

Wherever your intention goes, your energy flows. This means that once you set an intention to get well, and you TRULY want to, and you believe it, your powerful energy system will release the right hormones and antibodies to help you heal. Furthermore, it will also attract the right people, therapy, and support to help you heal.

Your power is your seventy, never let anything or anyone take your power away.

use your power

Now that you understand how powerful you are, practise manifesting what you desire. Start with something small and achievable, as this will build your confidence in your ability to manifest and create change.

Set an intention today to see a word, or a colour, or a type of dog, or a certain shape, or a make of car, or a flower, or whatever you wish. Make it something you don't see every day—pick just one thing. Now spend the day expecting it to show up. Stay present, or you might miss it.

If it didn't show up, don't get disheartened, it will when you're ready to believe it. Once you have mastered manifesting small things, you are ready to manifest bigger and better things for yourself and your life.

it's your time

It's time to heal your pain. Ask yourself, "Why am I in pain?" Whether your pain is emotional or physical, know that you don't have to have it in your life anymore. Know it's possible to heal all wounds through the power of your MindBody wisdom. If you are truly ready to stop this pattern of pain, then you can heal it now.

It's important to keep believing in the power of self-healing. Relate to yourself as someone who has the power to heal themselves, never doubt your power, because your power is the same power that created the universe.

You are that power!

How much do you believe you are worthy of true health and happiness? The more worthy you feel, the more committed you will be to keep practising healing yourself.

The more you heal, the more you will keep creating a life of health and happiness.

transform your pain into power

You are one of the special ones, because you are now ready for metamorphosis. You know that by going through the darkness of your pain, will allow you to experience your greatest light. This is your unique opportunity to turn your pain into your power!

If you're experiencing pain now, whether it be physical or emotional, know that it can be transformed into your gift. We grow and evolve through adversity and become a better version of ourselves because of it. Just like the friction of a grain of sand in an oyster shell creates a pearl, we need friction and agitation in life to create gems.

Although your current pain may feel all-encompassing, trust that it's a necessary pathway to your power. Once you find the gift within your suffering, you will shine so brightly that you will be a beacon of light for others.

It's your time to have a healthy, happy, and fulfilled life.

Enjoy x

what you can do next...

find your pathway from pain into power

Whatever path you choose next, know that you're not alone. I will help you every step of the way.

- **MindBody Transformation:** 1-2-1 with Jakkie

- **Mindbody Magic Bootcamp**: A transformational online course to help heal deep wounds and magically create a life you love.
  www.mindbodymagic.teachable.com/p/mindbodymagic

- **MindBody Journey:** An interactive course in a book to help you connect with your MindBody Wisdom.

- **Subscribe:** Join our community for ongoing support, inspiring blogs, monthly online group coaching, updates on live workshops and special offers.

visit: www.jakkietalmage.com
contact: jakkie@jakkietalmage.com

"

YOU MUST FIND THE PLACE INSIDE YOURSELF WHERE NOTHING IS IMPOSIBLE

"

DEEPAK CHOPRA

Printed in Great Britain
by Amazon

29395957R00066